GETTING TO KNOW
THE WORLD'S
GREATEST COMPOSERS

FRÉDÉRIC
CHOPIN

WRITTEN AND ILLUSTRATED BY MIKE VENEZIA

CONSULTANT

DONALD FREUND, PROFESSOR OF COMPOSITION, INDIANA UNIVERSITY SCHOOL OF MUSIC

CHILDREN'S PRESS®
A DIVISION OF GROLIER PUBLISHING
NEW YORK   LONDON   HONG KONG   SYDNEY
DANBURY, CONNECTICUT

Picture Acknowledgements
Photographs ©: Archives of the Chopin Society: 10, 13; Art Resource, NY: 28 top (Lauros-Giraudon/Musee de la Ville de Paris, Musee Carnavalet), 3, 14 (Giraudon), 6 (Scala), 11 (Tate Gallery); Bridgeman Art Library International Ltd., London/New York: 16, 17 (PFA107919 *The Midday Rest* by Franciszek Streitt, oil on panel/Phillips, The International Fine Art Auctioneers, UK.); Corbis-Bettmann: 32; Gamma-Liaison, Inc.: 31 top (Hulton Getty); Mary Evans Picture Library: 28 bottom (Explorer), 18 (Steve Rumney), 23, 31 bottom.

Colorist for illustrations: Kathy Hickey

Library of Congress Cataloging–in–Publication Data

Venezia, Mike.
 Frédéric Chopin / written and illustrated by Mike Venezia.
   p. cm. — (Getting to know the world's greatest composers)
 Summary: Describes the life and work of the nineteenth-century Polish composer who invented beautiful music for the piano and new ways of playing it.
  ISBN 0-516-21588-4 (lib. bdg.) 0-516-26534-2 (pbk.)
  1. Chopin, Frédéric, 1810-1849—Juvenile literature.
 2. Composers—Biography—Juvenile literature. [1. Chopin, Frédéric, 1810-1849. 2. Composers.] I. Title. II. Series:
 Venezia, Mike. Getting to know the world's greatest composers.
ML3930.C46V45 1999
786.2'092—dc21
[b]   99-13860
                           CIP

Portrait of Chopin, by Eugene Delacroix

Frédéric Chopin was born in 1810 in Zelazowa-Wola, Poland. Almost all his compositions were written just for the piano. Chopin wrote beautiful music for the piano and invented new ways of playing it.

Frédéric Chopin loved and understood music at a very early age. When he was about four years old, he liked to lie under the piano while his older sister, Louise, practiced. Sometimes he would burst into tears because he thought the music was so beautiful.

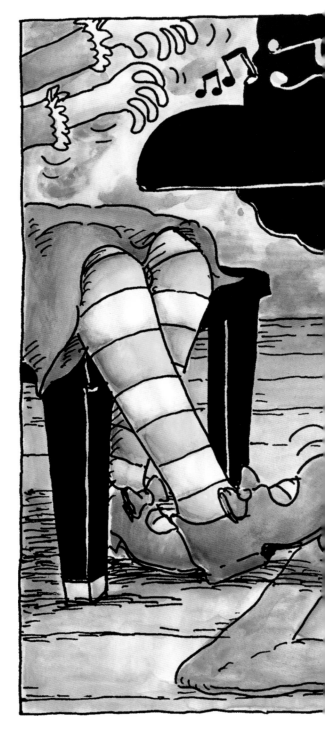

Wolfgang Amadeus Mozart

Frédéric soon began experimenting with the piano himself. His parents were amazed by how quickly their son learned things on his own.

When Frédéric was six years old, they decided to find him a teacher. Adalbert Zywny was Frédéric's first music teacher. He taught his new student basic piano skills. He also taught Frédéric a love for the music of such great composers from the past as Johann Sebastian Bach and Wolfgang Amadeus Mozart.

It wasn't long before everyone realized that
young Frédéric Chopin had a remarkable gift
for music. Frédéric once told his father that
it would be much easier for him to express
his feelings if they could be put into notes
of music.

Frédéric Chopin was a good student and listened to his teacher. But he enjoyed making up his own music more than anything else.

By the time Chopin was eight years old, some of his musical pieces had been published, and he had even given a public concert. At the concert, Frédéric was more worried about what the audience thought of his new velvet coat and collar than what they thought about his music. As it turned out, the audience loved Chopin's music.

Frédéric's parents, Justine and Nicolas Chopin

Mr. and Mrs. Chopin were proud of Frédéric's musical talent. They made sure he had an excellent education in other areas too. Mr. Chopin taught French to the children of wealthy families in Warsaw, Poland's capital city. He knew the importance of education and good manners.

The Chopins became friends with many of Warsaw's most interesting people. Frédéric got used to having dukes, countesses, poets, authors, and artists visiting his home all the time.

Frédéric at the piano as a young boy

*W*hile growing up, Frédéric Chopin was always polite, well mannered, and concerned about dressing neatly. Because of this, some people think he must have had a boring childhood. But Frédéric was like lots of other kids. One of his favorite things to do was ride horses, although he later wrote that he wasn't very good at it.

Cartoons drawn by Frédéric as a young boy

He also had a good sense of humor. Frédéric drew funny pictures of his teachers, schoolmates, and friends that kept everyone laughing. He liked ice-skating, and he had lots of girlfriends, too.

Poland was having all kinds of problems when Frédéric Chopin was growing up. The biggest problem was that Poland was always being taken over by more powerful countries. One of Poland's neighbors, Russia, decided it would like to keep a part of Poland for itself.

When Frédéric was fifteen years old, he was asked to give a performance for Czar Alexander I, the ruler of Russia. The czar gave Frédéric a diamond ring after the concert. That was an exciting moment for Frédéric Chopin.

Czar Alexander I of Russia

Chopin was becoming well known and appreciated. But he was also becoming bothered that the Polish people were being bossed around by outsiders.

Chopin's teenage years were very important. He was getting his ideas together on how he felt about his country, his music, and his future. He especially learned a lot from going on summer vacations with his family. In the countryside of Poland,

The Midday Rest, a painting by Franciszek Streitt showing the Polish countryside in the 1800s

Frédéric Chopin saw the hardworking Polish peasants and heard their music.

People had been singing and dancing to this music for hundreds of years. Frédéric got lots of ideas for his own music from these trips.

One popular folk dance Frédéric learned about was the mazurka. The music for this dance can be lively and exciting or sweetly sad. It was an important part of the lives of Polish peasants. People felt proud of their homeland when they heard and danced mazurkas. They knew they had something of their own that even a bossy czar couldn't take from them.

Eastern European folk dancing

Frédéric Chopin ended up composing more than fifty of his own mazurkas. He added his own special touches, and mazurkas became some of his most popular works. Chopin's Mazurka in B-flat Major, Op.7, No.1, is a good example of how he captured the spirit, fun, and excitement of Polish life in his music.

*a*fter Frédéric finished high school and music college, he traveled to other countries in Europe to give performances. After a few very successful trips, Frédéric and his family and teachers thought there would be better opportunities for him in cities like Vienna, Austria, and Paris, France. Music was much more popular in these cities than it was in Warsaw.

On November 2, 1830, Frédéric Chopin decided to leave Poland to make his fortune. He didn't know it then, but he would never return to the country he loved so much.

*a*t the time Chopin left home, Poland
wasn't the only country with problems.
People all over Europe were getting fed
up with outside governments trying to take
over their countries or having their own
uncaring rulers run their lives. It was a
dangerous time to be traveling.

Even so, Frédéric continued on to Paris.
Along the way, he heard shocking news.
A group of Polish citizens had started a
rebellion to throw out the Russian czar
and his soldiers. Frédéric was upset, and
was worried about the safety of his friends
and family.

Street fighting in Warsaw, Poland, during the 1830 revolt against Russian rule

He became inspired to compose one of his most exciting and powerful pieces, the Etude in C Minor (also known as the *Revolutionary Etude*). This piece is filled with the spirit of rebellion. In parts, it seems to explode with rushing piano sounds! All of Chopin's hopes for his country come alive in this amazing piano piece.

When Frédéric Chopin arrived in Paris, he couldn't believe how busy and exciting the city was. Paris was filled with famous authors, poets, artists—and especially musicians and composers. Frédéric was welcomed right away. He became best friends with one of the most famous pianists of all time, Franz Liszt.

Liszt was a piano virtuoso. A virtuoso is a person who does something better than almost anyone else in the world. Chopin was surprised to find out that virtuosos would sometimes challenge each other to see who was the best. Audiences loved these contests. Once Frédéric watched Liszt and another virtuoso have a play-off.

In the past, Frédéric had given concerts as a way of making money and becoming better known. But even though he was one of the best pianists ever, Chopin never really enjoyed playing for big audiences. In fact, he was usually terrified of performing!

In Paris, people weren't that interested in Chopin's concerts because Chopin wasn't as big a show-off and didn't play as loudly as other piano virtuosos. That was just fine with Frédéric. Now he was able to spend more time composing and playing for

small groups of friends. Chopin also found he could make lots of money giving piano lessons to members of the wealthy families he met in Paris.

George Sand dressed in men's clothing

One evening, when Frédéric was at a party, Franz Liszt introduced him to an unusual woman author named George Sand. George Sand's books were very popular at the time. They were filled with new ideas and different ways of looking at life. George sometimes dressed in men's clothes, and even smoked cigars!

George Sand smoking a cigar while watching Franz Liszt play the piano

At first, Frédéric thought George Sand was just too weird to become friends with, but after he got to know her, he fell deeply in love. For the next ten years, Frédéric Chopin and George Sand had one of the most famous romances of the century. It was during these years that Chopin composed most of his greatest works.

Chopin composed so many different types of music that it's sometimes hard to keep them all straight. Some of his most popular pieces are dances, like mazurkas, polonaises, and waltzes. Most of these pieces weren't really meant to be danced to. They were more about the spirit of dancing and the excitement of the times.

He also wrote etudes. These are short studies used for teaching piano. But Chopin turned them into much more than simple studies. In the *Revolutionary Etude,* for example, you can almost feel Chopin's fiery temper. Chopin's Waltz in D Major, Op.64, No.1, is so quick and breathless that everyone calls it the "Minute Waltz" (although no one can play it in a minute!).

The nocturnes are another popular category. The word *nocturne* means "night piece." Chopin's nocturnes are slow and dreamy in feeling. They're great to listen to when you want to relax and just think about things.

Chopin composing his preludes

Frédéric Chopin in 1849

*U*nfortunately, Frédéric Chopin had poor health for much of his life. When he and George Sand broke up, he slowly became worse. Chopin wrote a few more pieces and gave some concerts until he felt too weak to do any more. He died quietly in Paris in 1849.

No matter which category of his music they listen to, most people find Frédéric Chopin's compositions to be some of the most original, sensitive, and beautiful music ever.